I0470309

The Economics of Economic Organization

A Communications-Cost Approach to Optimum Economic Cooperation

by

William T. White

authorHOUSE®

AuthorHouse™
1663 Liberty Drive
Bloomington, IN 47403
www.authorhouse.com
Phone: 1-800-839-8640

First published by AuthorHouse   2/18/2010

ISBN: 978-1-4490-7508-8 (sc)
ISBN: 978-1-4490-9222-1 (e)

Library of Congress Control Number: 2010900968

This book is printed on acid-free paper.

Preface

IF YOU WORK FOR, INVEST in, or are a customer of an economic organization, the chances are that you think that the organization's policies and practices are stupid and wrong for you, wrong for the organization itself and wrong for society as a whole.

Also, the chances are that you are surprised and concerned about the financial crisis of the fall of 2008.

You read that we need "transparency" but you can't find the word anywhere in your college economics textbook.

You're probably right to be concerned,
But, it's not your organization's fault.
It's not your fault either.
It's my fault, because....

....I'm an economist and we economists have failed to develop a rigorous theory of optimum economic organization. Yet, such theory is much needed as a basis for rational, persuasive and ethically defensible ideologies and business practices for a modern economy. In particular, economic theory has failed to recognize that economic organizations at levels between the individual and the nation-state exist to reduce the costs of communication. Economic theory also largely ignores the natural links from truth and open information to the communication that shapes and ultimately limits economic cooperation. And while the business and political worlds have newly discovered the importance of "transparency", the word remains ill defined and rarely found in rigorous economic theory and economics textbooks. In consequence, important and long admired elements of our economy, especially in finance, are loaded with secrets and lies about those secrets.

The changes needed in economics are at the level of basic postulates and may at first seem trivial. However, after the almost complete failure of monetarist economics and market fundamentalism in the worst recession since the Great Depression, major changes at the core of economics could be essential to the survival of economics, both as a guide to national and international prosperity and as a rational academic discipline.

This book is a retirement project. It is written now because it is needed now, and at last I have had time to consider again questions and problems that have long troubled me but were put aside in a career in which the study of economics had to be combined with other occupations. I do not write, "regrettably combined", however. It is my work in a multitude of organizational settings that has shown me the need for a major expansion in economic theory to encompass economic organizations, particularly at levels between the individual and the nation state: the businesses, universities, hospitals, unions, economic elements of governments and the many others organizations that actually provide most of the output and most of the jobs in an economy.

From the beginning of my study of economics I enjoyed its pure theory the most, but noticed that it had very little to do with the economic world in which I lived. My economics textbooks and classroom lectures were mostly about individuals and their buying, selling, investing and other economic activity in markets. Yet, I and just about everyone I knew worked in an economic organization, bought from economic organizations, invested in economic organizations and, with minor exceptions, involved organizations in whatever other economic things we did.

As the years went by, the reality that economic activity was mainly organized economic activity did not change much, except that I had personal experience with organizations of many different types in many different settings. Organizations with which I became involved at the executive level included those which were large and those which were small; financial and operational; military and civilian; religious and non-religious; governmental at local, state, national and international levels; academic and non-academic; profit-making and not-for-profit; those in totalitarian economies and those in largely free market economies; those, like China and Las Vegas, that were fast-growing and those of the

Great Depression that were stagnant or dying. Yet, there seemed always to be common principles that applied to economic organizations, whatever their specific natures and functions.

Possibly influenced at least in part by a U.S. Supreme Court decision that corporations had to be treated legally as individuals[1], most economists and economic theory largely abstracted from economic organizations. Microeconomics deals almost entirely with individuals, or organizations treated as individuals, using markets. Macroeconomics is concerned with economic policies and practices of nation-states. Neither is concerned with the economic entities at levels between the individual and the nation state.

The development of a rigorous and useful economics of middle-level economic organization brings with it a broad and important reconsideration of economic organization in general. Mainstream economic theory must recognize that economic organization is a necessary complement of markets at any level of economic cooperation, from individuals, through middle-level entities and on to economic elements of nation-states and the international economy as well.

There has long been a debate in economics, and in all the other social sciences and philosophy as well, about the need for and source of restrictions on the pursuit of self-interest for the common good. Those who emphasize this need largely regard the retreat from self-interest as a compromise to gain order and avoid "war of all against all," to use Thomas Hobbes' wording. This book argues that rational self-seeking individuals will use economic organization in combination with markets to gain the benefits of economic cooperation with other individuals. It thus abets rather than compromises self-interest. Any individual behavior that is responsive to any other guidance or any forced other behavior can but depart from the optimum use of economic organization in economic cooperation. Stated another way, emphasis on the benefits for individuals of economic cooperation and the truthful communication that makes it possible is not derived from religious or cultural code of ethics, but is instead economically rational and simply "good business" for self-seeking individuals. Adherence to this position, which should be at the core of mainstream economics, makes possible a unified economic theory.

Chapter 1 is primarily methodological, setting forth the fundamentals of an extension of economic theory that is based on economic man's rational use of economic organization. It is based on marginal analysis, not by a central planning authority but by individuals responding to their own knowledge and circumstances, the familiar and trusted tool used for centuries. Chapter 2 covers selected schools of economic thought and one economist-philosopher, James Buchanan, that have recognized at least that economic organization, including contracting, is an essential companion of markets in effecting economic cooperation. The schools of thought discussed successively are law and economics; institutional economics; and Catholic economics; Additionally there is a brief discussion of Buchanan's contractual approach and of a current (2009) attempt to combine Keynesian economics with psychology to explain individual economic behavior that is outside market optimization. Most, but not all of the other approaches discussed, recognize economic organization but generally narrow its use to supporting socially necessary compromises of economic-man behavior.

Chapter 3 considers small utopian communities showing recognition of the relationship between economic cooperation and the communication that is possible in a small community of like-minded people. For economic theory, the dreams of utopian communities were more important than their failed realities. The chapter discusses the short life span of most utopian communities. On balance, it appears that failure of utopian communities is the result more of too little rather than too much emphasis on economic purpose. Thus the community that lasted the longest by far was that at Oneida, New York, which evolved from a primarily religious group to a completely economic purpose prospering with, and to the extent of, the change.

The need to revise economics to recognize communications costs and economic organization extends to all parts of economics and its full treatment is beyond any reasonable scope of this book, which seeks mainly to introduce as briefly as possible a new approach in economic theory. However, It is useful to present selected examples of the scope and depth of the needed changes in Microeconomics (Chapter 4), Macroeconomics (Chapter 5), and the Economics of international trade and finance (Chapter 6). Chapter 7 is dedicated to financial markets and reaches the conclusion that the long history of laws and regulations of financial market had important results opposite to those intended.

I owe my second look at truth to my wife. Lola B. White, who gives it general importance but guided me to the economic principle that truth and open information are critically important but oft-neglected essentials to economic cooperation. For the idea that nation-state economics might be incorporated in a consistent microeconomics I am indebted to Svetozar Pejovich, professor emeritus at Texas A&M, whose denial of the usefulness of macroeconomics as it is led me to a theory of economic organization that can unify economic theory in general. I am also deeply indebted to the Mid-20th century economics graduate faculty of Georgetown University for my lasting interest in ideal economic organizations and the need to identify and develop a rigorous theory about them.

I leave it to financial crisis of the fall of 2008 and the content of the book itself to explain why it needed to be written.

1
The Basics

ECONOMISTS LONG AGO PRODUCED ELABORATE and persuasive doctrine showing that individuals, in working and trading in free markets wholly to maximize their own well-being, also provide maximum benefit to society as a whole. The supporting theory explicitly or implicitly assumed that markets were competitive and that buyers and sellers would be fully and costlessly informed. Because these assumptions match reality only in part, the facts of the world have not always, or even usually, agreed with the postulates and findings of their derived ideologies. Nevertheless, beginning in the enlightenment, classical economic theory has provided the idealizations that underlie rational market capitalism and its laws, customs and practices.

But the same cannot be said of economic organizations that support, complement and augment markets in creating and sustaining economic cooperation. Furthermore, there is almost no economic theory at all treating economic organizations at levels between the individual and the nation-state, even though these organizations produce most of the output and employ most of the work force in free capitalist countries. Without a rigorous and accepted theory of economic organization, there is no defendable ideology and business practice common to those about markets. In the absence of a respected theory of economic organization, there is an all-too-common practice of using market theory to justify anti-cooperative behavior, particularly by market fundamentalists. One prominent result is 21st Century confusion about appropriate, just and useful behavior of the leaderships of financial institutions.

A central tenet of this book is that the essential purpose of economic organization is the reduction of the communications costs and uncertainties of economic cooperation. The relatively recent attention to transactions costs includes communications costs, but usually more or less as an aside and not in the central role they require in the analysis of economic organizations, the task of this book.

In mainstream economics communications costs have been included explicitly or implicitly among "frictions" that might slow but not alter economic outcomes. An alternative presentation of the same treatment is to include communications costs among "short run" factors that disappear in the "long run". Not even the penetrating remark by J.M. Keynes, essentially the creator of macroeconomics, that the "long-run" cannot be anything more than a series of "short runs" has served to eliminate the essentially useless shortrun-longrun dichotomy from either economic theory or real-world business parlance.

Many market defenders argue that free markets can and should provide the only effective and just method of coordinating economic activity. However, even the most ardent of market champions, Milton Friedman among them[2], have recognized specifically that markets require some supporting economic organization, such as agreements on where and when to meet for trading, property rights, a trading language, an accepted money and numerous other institutions, laws, rules, and governing customs that make trading in markets practical. Although organizational support of markets varies widely, the dependence of all markets on some type of organization is absolute. And just as in organized sports, effective competition requires cooperation in following organizationally agreed rules, whatever they are.

The role of economic organization with respect to markets is not limited to the support of markets. Rather, economic organizations are full complements of markets, including substituting for them in coordinating economic activity of individuals. Like labor and capital, factors of production in classical production theory, neither markets nor economic organization can function without the other in coordinating economic activity. Because they can be substitutes for one another as well as complements, the optimum combination of markets and economic organizations is achieved when the benefits gained by added expenditures on one of them is equal to the benefits of the same expenditure on the other. It is important to recognize that this optimization is individually oriented, as it must be because only individuals know their utility functions, risk preferences, and the degree to which they wish to optimize the optimization, given its communications costs Stated more completely and in the language of economics, an optimum is reached when the marginal benefits of expanding market activity and marginal benefits of expanding economic organization are equal to each other and equal also to both the marginal gain in value of the resulting economic coordination and the marginal costs of communication. Finally, equal marginal returns extends across the many dimensions of expansion or contraction, so that, for example, marginal returns from expanding a product line are equal to those from expanding a customer base demographically. For the many pundits who see the economic system and policy as a matter of choice between markets and government, which is at least in major part an economic organization, their insistencies are simply a waste of time, neither option being possible alone either theoretically or practicably.

An important part of economic organization is its use to reduce and/or eliminate uncertainty through contracts that are essentially exchanges of promises. The real world closely mirrors the theoretical essentiality of economic coordination by a combination of markets and the contractual component of economic organization, useful even when available data do not permit buying and selling based on expected values. A university department chair cannot use the world-wide academic personnel market each day to determine who will teach each department class section that day. A major manufacturing firm cannot use auction markets daily to determine who will fill each position in the firm, or which other companies will provide each product input or how any of the many other daily processes will be coordinated. Instead, markets largely will be used in conjunction with economic organization by extending the terms markets reach in time, sales areas and in the many other dimensions covered by contracts or other organizational arrangements. Organization in its contracting form can provide usable stability and a usable degree of certainty in economic cooperation even when there is a high degree of uncertainty without it.

Also in the real world, organizations among individuals to improve their cooperation are not always completely economic in nature and purpose. For mixed organizations such as government, the economics of organization like the rest of economic theory are cogent and useful insofar as mixed organizations are economic and no further. With this covenant the flexible and vigorous market for economic organizations fits rationally into the main body of microeconomic theory and much of the rest of classical economics.

Mention was made earlier that rational and persuasive economic theory of competitive markets provided a basis for prevailing and successful market culture. Similarly, a rational and persuasive economic theory of economic organization is needed to support a productive culture for economic organizations. There are two critically important elements of the culture that devolve naturally from theory recognizing that economic organizations exist to reduce communications costs for individuals. The first is the need for truth and open information, "transparency", in current business language. The second is that economic organizations must yield priority to the individuals who create and sustain them. This special subsidiarty required of rationally used economic organizations is part of the principle that self-seeking by individuals produces optimum societal outcomes. Rational individuals insist on a demanding level of subsidiarity of economic organizations with which they have meaningful relationships. It can be simply stated. Each and every individual must derive a net benefit from each and every relationship with economic organizations.

From the point of view of self-seeking individuals buying and selling in markets, economics has long persisted in the deductive argument that productive resources, including labor, will not be left unemployed. But in reality free market capitalism has been plagued by repeated periods of significant unemployment of resources, with unemployment of labor understandably commanding the most concern and attention. The assumption of classical economics were that unused resources would be instantly known to entrepreneurs, who would see profit in using them and promptly put them into use. There was no recognition of the communications costs of knowing about and acting to employ unused resources. Therefore, classical economics had no explanations or solutions for recessions. The rational statement about employment of idle resources is that they will be used to the point at which benefits justify the costs, with the costs reduced as much as possible by economic organization.

The recurrence of business slumps, and especially the Great Depression, which spread from the United States to the rest of free-market countries, led to popular support for and political adoption of several kinds and degrees of economic organization at the nation-state level. The systems used varied from the total command of fascist and communist centrally planned economies to macroeconomic fiscal and monetary policies in political democracies, essentially managed with feedback techniques. The different systems shared common economic goals of reducing unemployment, stabilizing prices and maintaining currency values, and to do so without stifling economic growth. There was little if any recognition that these movements constituted a giant leap into economic organization at a nation-state level to achieve economic cooperation manifestly not available from markets alone. Economic theory should have recognized, but did not, that individuals could not see through the complexities of modern industrial society and had therefore collectively created economic organization at the nation-state level to effect economic cooperation. There was little if any recognition of the need for truth and open information that would have followed rigorous theory built on the axiom that economic organization exists to reduce communications costs. Indeed over the decades the United States Federal Reserve has developed strict secrecy systems for its deliberations that are unparalleled even in military history and effectively prevent needed inputs by individuals into those deliberations.

Three-quarters of a century after the stock market crash of 1929 that ushered in the Great Depression, there is widespread recognition of the need for "transparency" in financial institutions, private, governmental, and combinations of the two such as Fannie May and Freddie Mac, both of which failed in 2008. But there is no widespread agreement on the full meaning of "transparency", little use of the term in economic theory and no close connection with a theory of economic organizations and their communications purpose as here articulated.

As will be shown further on, there are major inconsistencies between microeconomics and macroeconomics, and some of these inconsistencies are at the level of basic postulates. Many of them disappear with recognition of the costs of communications and the role of economic organization in limiting those costs. As a beginning in applying the theory here to nation-state economies, it is clear that macroeconomic attempts to stimulate investment nationally presume an informed consent that is not necessarily or even usually present. But there can be sufficient public agreement on a smaller scale, as for example in utopian communities and at state level when Louisiana Governor Huey Long, with strong public support, built needed bridges to use otherwise unemployed labor and thus significantly to moderate the Louisiana effects of the Great Depression.

The nature and importance of the needed but largely missing theory of economic organization becomes clear in a return to basics, beginning with the importance of economic cooperation. Since the beginning of time, individuals have been heavily dependent for their material well being on their economic cooperation with one another. Very few of us could survive alone in the wilderness for more than a few weeks. Those who could survive longer surely would be using resources and learning consciously or unconsciously passed on to them through intergenerational cooperation as part of our heritage.

And by and large the quality of our lives from any level of living improves when our cooperation expands and worsens when cooperation declines. While in reality some cooperation among individuals can have negative results, an economic theory of economic organization can most usefully assume, as microeconomics long has for other inputs of production, that the economic tool of cooperation benefits individuals in all dimensions of expansion, but with increasing costs and decreasing returns.

Economics has long recognized and analyzed in elegant detail trading in money-implemented free markets as a major method of interpersonal economic cooperation. Most of us readily understand that individuals and countries can benefit by selling goods that they can produce more cheaply than others (absolute advantage) and buying goods that others can produce more cheaply than they can. But even if one person or country can produce everything more cheaply than another, there is still mutual benefit from trading between the two, which is not so readily recognized. In the 1820's English businessman and economist David Ricardo showed that trading is mutually beneficial even if one party has no absolute advantage for any product. All that is required for mutually profitable trade between two entities is that the advantages that one has over the other differ for different products.

The Ricardo logic applies to the different wants of different individuals. As long as the patterns of wants of individuals differ, trade among them also is mutually beneficial. Theoretically, if there were no communications costs, every individual on Earth could find advantage in trading with every other individual on Earth. But there are communications costs and they set rational limits to trading. We need to understand, appreciate and protect the great benefits to mankind from their great reduction over the last century and the resulting increase in economic cooperation.

Just as markets require organizational support, so economic organizations require market support. Employers and potential employees bargain about compensation and working conditions before hiring is done, and most already-hired employees keep an eye on employment possibilities elsewhere. Employers at least intermittently evaluate employees and consider options ranging from changes in pay to termination or promotion of employees. Producing entities in a complex economy contract with both suppliers and customers at particular prices. They do not try to capture the gains from change in market prices unless those gains exceed the communications costs of realizing them.

There is an optimum mixture of buying and selling in markets and economic organizations for each individual in each of his quests for a better life. And at their limits markets are organizational and economic organization at its limit becomes a type of market, being simply a continuation of buying and selling from momentary to a more stable arrangement in one dimension or another to reduce communications costs. Economic theory must recognize also that individuals can and will spontaneously create and sustain or abandon economic organizations wherever and whenever it benefits them to do so. Spontaneous changes in markets and in economic organizations, including their demise when they are no longer useful, must be allowed to occur to reach and sustain equilibrium in the multi-faceted, multi-dimensional market for spontaneous economic organizations. Finally, individuals must be permitted to establish and maintain the nature and degree of their participation in both markets and economic organizations.

The need for a major change in the treatment of communications costs in economics is made pressing by the revolution in communications technology of the last half century. Born of necessity in World War II, and spurred especially by computer development and the invention of the transistor, the technological revolution in communications, in the broad nature of Joseph Schumpeter's "innovation," has been incorporated in the economies of every country on Earth. The resulting effects on human cooperation, thus far and into the future, are rivaled in all history only by those of the fifteenth century introduction into European civilization of Gutenberg's movable type, itself a radical improvement in human communication.

The previously stated organizational requirement for truth is not derived from religious values or some other normative abandonment of self-interest. It is instead simply "good business" adopted by self-seeking individuals recognizing the economic benefits to them of cooperation with others. A practical corollary is that information security systems are in general anti-social and anti-economic striking at the core of economic cooperation. If they are used at all by rational individuals, they will be required, as a condition of their existence, to justify the cost of them in reduced economic cooperation.

The second stated requirement of a rational and rigorous theory of economic organization, that organizations be philosophically subsidiary to individuals, also must be viewed in a demanding way. No economic organization can be considered too big to be allowed to fail. As part of this principle of special subsidiarity, economic organizations must be ever changing, flexible, and responsive to changes in individuals' needs and wants. Economic organizations cannot survive by benefiting only a majority of the individuals using them. They must meet the higher standard of benefiting each and every individual each and every time and each and every way they are used. Otherwise, individuals should and will terminate or appropriately modify and or limit the individuals' use of the organization involved. Also, individuals must be flexible, especially in regard to career changes, retirement ages and non-wage compensation.

The unified theory of economics offered here treats nation-state economic action, the domain of macroeconomics, as just a special case of economic organization in the interest of individuals. Gone are such constructs as the "fallacy of composition" used to "explain" how truisms derived from individual experience are sometimes completely reversed when applied to the nation-state, which is comprised of the totality of individuals. Added is the realization that national money is but another element of economic organization, sharing any influence it may have on the real economy of goods and services with all other elements of economic organization, including especially close money substitutes, recognized as such or not.

The ideological derivatives of the theory that treats economic organization as a tool of communication and economic cooperation are simple and practical, even though they often employ new terminology. Thus, a firm with an increased number of water leaks can put another plumber into its work force to handle the increase, an organizational solution, or it can "outsource" some leak repairs by calling an independent plumber, a market solution. The particular mixture of outsourcing (market) and in-house plumbers (organizational) the firm will be using at any particular time, as well as the total amount spent on plumbing is determined by switching between the two methods until the marginal communications costs of them are equal and equal to the marginal benefit from plumbing expenditures. It is important that this solution be regarded as rationally determined on economic grounds alone and completely in accord with the self-interest of the business involved. Therefore, any departure from the solution for normative reasons is economically non-optimum.

There are many dimensions in the expansion of cooperation available to managers. They can continue to function as they are, thus expanding in the time dimension. They can expand both production and sales into additional locations, domestic or foreign, adopt new types and/or models of product, attract new customer age groups, and/or use numerous other dimensions of expansion. And again they will shift resources among dimensions until the returns from the last dollar spent on each are all equal. Obviously, computation of the optimum allocation of resources in accordance with the socialist planned economy model is extremely complex and proven impractical wherever tried. But no such computation is necessary if the spontaneous creation and survival of economic organization are free and competitive and subsidiary to individuals. As is true of goods markets, optimization by individuals in the combination of markets and economic organizations, however complicated it may be, produces a result that is optimum for the individuals involved and for society as a whole.

There has long been support for the view that inter-individual cooperation is consistent with selfish individualism. In this view, the desire to cooperate with others is part of the individual and is in his nature (as God made him in the view of many). This is in accord with the natural order philosophies of John Locke, Adam Smith, and all the others who treat man as a social being that naturally does all he can for himself, both in competitive markets and in cooperating with others through economic organizations. There is no reason to deny that individuals can do this just as well as they make current market choices that are optimum for them. A different view is that pursuit of self-interest does not contain cooperation with other individuals and must be compromised by an imposed order or code of behavior to gain the benefits of economic cooperation. Those who essentially adopted the latter view include Thomas Hobbes and all the others who, at least in part, see individuals' efforts to better themselves as leading inevitably to Hobbes "war of all against all," avoidable only by the imposition of a top-down socioeconomic structure providing order and social cooperation.

Economic organizations have a special cost that has important policy implications. The formation and survival of mutually beneficial economic organizations are based, consciously or unconsciously, on mutual acceptance of assumptions about the future or movement in any other dimension. These assumptions cannot be perfect, and there are increasing costs from the growing differences between founding assumptions and reality as it emerges with movement in time or any other dimension. Further, the participants involved in an economic organization and its founding agreements have some control over at least part of emerging reality that can be used to keep it in agreement with assumptions on which the economic organization is based. This means that participants in economic organizations can at least partially control the costs of organization simply by keeping their promises, be they overt or implied.

On an overall basis and especially with reference to its core, conventional economics has little to offer in anticipating and understanding the effects of the great improvement in human communications and its relationship to economic organizations. The options that individuals have to cooperate by creating and sustaining economic organizations are not part of the basic postulates of microeconomics, but they need to be. This task is begun in Chapter 4 with a new look at supply and demand that distinguishes between useful abstraction from reality and theoretical error common in mainstream market models. That error is in the assumption of competition without recognizing the communications costs that create those markets rather than ubiquitous monopoly rationally expected of economic man.

For its part, macroeconomics presumes that individuals cannot see through to final effects, and therefore posits that such changes as those in the quantity of money and resulting interest rates and price levels can affect output and employment. This cannot occur if there were no communications costs and prices therefore could be automatically indexed and inflation made perfect and all pervasive, or nearly so. Supporting this statement, U.S. prices have multiplied by a factor of more than 12 in the last half-century without destroying the economy. Over time, the economy has made inflation almost all pervasive. Also, the erratic but repetitive near collapse of several national monies in Southeast Asia in the 1980's did not affect output and employment in the countries involved nearly as much as would be expected from macroeconomics, largely because international companies spontaneously used economic organization to keep the wheels turning with non-local monies, money substitutes and sophisticated modern barter. But, as with microeconomics, there is no adequate and consistent treatment of rational, self-seeking economic organizations in macroeconomics.

As will be seen in Chapters 4,5, and 6, the market for economic organization is naturally dynamic and broad in scope. The mixtures of economic organization and markets as individuals seek to increase the benefits of economic cooperation are continually changing, and this is a very important point for economic theory. Specifically, the much-used distinction between short-run and long run effects is a poor approach in explaining the market for economic organizations. For example, cost analysis in the typical first text in economics treats as part of the total cost of a good as fixed on the argument that for some unspecified length of time certain capital assets cannot be changed. One widely respected and much used text even uses three types of capital assets: variable, semi-fixed and fixed. But this is an illusion. While the existence or non-existence of a factory may take time to change, the use of the factory and whether or not it is used at all is a variable receiving consideration on a continuous basis

In respect to his critically important variable, business investment spending, Keynes recognized two types of uncertainties concerning investment spending. One type includes those for which available data allow the calculation of expected values and rational investment decisions based on those expected values. The second type includes those potential investments for which available data do not permit such computations. Recognizing the reality of investments of the second type, Keynes attributed them to "animal spirits", outside economic explanations perhaps toward a behavioral approach. But cogent theory of economic organization offers a better explanation. Individuals can rationally make investments of the second type using economic organization's contracts and implied contracts to erase even risks that are unknown. A somewhat subtle example is one in which an event of unknown probability is so valuable to an investor organizationally that he will repeatedly invest in attempts to realize it. This last point can be made clear in what might be called the threshold theory of gaming.

Consider the case of an entrepreneur who must make a $400,000 payment to the IRS by Monday morning or be put into bankruptcy or even jailed. Assume that he has

$40,000 at present, which he will lose if he fails to make the $400,000 payment on Monday. One rational course of action for him is to go to Las Vegas and start betting the $40,000 following a rule that he will quit the tables if and when his stake reaches $400,000 allowing him to continue in business. If he goes broke without ever having reached $400,000 he is no worse off than he would have been if he did not gamble the $40,000. This is the exact opposite of the conservative visitor to Las Vegas who sets aside an amount he is willing to lose and follows a policy of gambling until his stake is all lost, which will happen inevitably. Generalizing, entrepreneurs can and will take unknowable risks on investments that, if successful, allow them to make an important organizational change in their futures. And they rationally will repeat this type of action even after losses.

Consider also that because of uncertainties many businesses refuse to make investments that do not return the total investment within five years, which means that they expect a return of approximately fifteen percent per year compounded. One effect of this is unresponsiveness of business investment spending to lowered interest rates, even if they are halved, say from six percent to three percent. When returns on investments are both uncertain and highly variable, it is not rational to invest all available funds is one proposition that promises a slightly better return than other investments. Instead, the rational investor will diversify investments into say five propositions, expecting that with variation unlimited on the high side while losses on the low side are limited to the amount invested, at least one of the investments will provide exceptional returns more than covering losses on the others.

2
Related Treatments of Economic Organization

THE NEED TO DEVELOP A better economics of economic organization has been recognized meaningfully by others. Most of these other treatments sought not to treat middle-level economic organizations *per se* but instead attempted to explain and/or justify departures from economic-man behavior, usually for the sake of order or for other social objectives. Away from the mainstream in economics are four smaller branches of economics, one economist/philosopher, and a 2009 book that seeks to combine economics and psychology to explain the current economy. Each of these does treat economic organization sufficiently to require at least a brief discussion here. The branches are: (1) the economics of planned economies and in particular its "computopia" versions, a dream of a computer-directed centralized management in totally planned economies; (2) Institutional economics, both the original version, long associated with the name of John R. Commons, and the "new institutional economics"; (3) the law and economics movement prominently associated with the University of Chicago and George Mason University and (4) Catholic economics, especially as articulated in the Depart of Economics at Georgetown University's mid-20th Century search for the ideal economic organization. The individual whose writings are particularly relevant to economic organization is the philosopher-economist James Buchanan, who has been associated with several universities including most prominently George Mason University, but with important differences from its law and economics orientation He also has made significant contributions to new institutional economics and done so in a way that relates closely with the emphasis on individuals of this book.

Each of the four smaller branches of economics has its own characteristics, advantages and limitations, but they have in common one fatal omission: the failure to assume formally and rigorously that the essential purpose of economic organizations is the reduction in communications costs of self-seeking individuals. Furthermore, while, they all have recognized economic organization's role in economic cooperation, all treat cooperation as a necessary compromise of economic-man behavior rather than an integral part of individual maximization using both markets and economic organization.

Recognizing formally that economic organizations exist to reduce communications costs has two special theoretical consequences. The first is that communications costs can be treated in microeconomic just as other costs are treated, extending that theory rigorously to economic organizations. The second is that the normative introduction of non-economic sources of organization that is often seen as a needed ethical compromise with self-seeking individualism, can but depart from the optimum in economic cooperation. While non-economic organization has its own worth, attempts to incorporate it into an economics of organization is essentially over-determination.

Beginning further discussion of the types of economics that have treated economic organizations specifically, there is little purpose in adding much to the copious but now dated writings in the long dispute between purist defenders of free markets capitalism and the equally purist advocates of centrally planned and directed economies, be they Marxist, fascist or otherwise economically dictatorial. Once communications cost are recognized, neither economic system in the pure form usually defended by its most ardent advocates is practicable, or even theoretically defensible. Almost all economies are mixed, despite the worldwide failures of national economic planning, "good planning" remains a widely respected political requirement of state and local governance, as indeed it should be. Mention should be made of Friedrich Hayek's discussions of the use of knowledge and the special advantages in that respect of individuals over government or other economic planners.[3]

Older institutional economics, even to include labor economics, is fundamentally descriptive and intentionally so. Descriptive work in institutional economics, once very popular and respected because of its emphasis on persons, is almost impossible because of its lack of adequately and consistently designed terminology normally provided by theory. Thus, descriptions of the roles and actions of one or another of the so-called robber barons or labor leaders in their glory, such as John D. Rockefeller and John L. Lewis, can be good reading, but they are not economics, despite discerning work such as John Kenneth Galbraith's *New Industrial State.*

The new institutional economics, which no longer is really new, recognizes that optimum economic coordination requires a combination of individual action in markets and economic organizations. It tends usually to see economic organizations as products of market experience, sometimes with appreciable normative content, holding that market outcomes are those that "ought to be", just because they happened. This is in sharp contrast with the view here that there is spontaneous but rational creation of economic organizations by self-seeking individuals using them to reduce communications costs and keep themselves subsidiary to the individuals that create and sustain them. On balance, the new economic institutionalism sees economic organization as a tenet of culture that is rational but also a governing compromise of economic-man behavior.

For the approach of this work, the law and economics movement is especially interesting. There are of course differences in the positions taken by advocates but there is also a degree of consistency that is rare in both economics and law. F. H. Buckley's book *Just Exchange*[4] provides a useful and relatively current (2005) source of views on several matters discussed in this work. Buckley's experience as associate dean and foundation professor at George Mason University and also his service as director of the George Mason Law and Economics Center have given his book special credibility in respect to the law and economics views on economic organizations.

In general, the law and economics movement does recognize that markets must be mixed with some sort of economic organization, giving it substantially more importance than is implied by classical market theory as already cited. Buckley argues that organization is needed to provide ethical guidance for rational and just capitalism. Buckley characterizes this input as normative, therefore to be provided essentially as a matter of faith. He further argues, in agreement with new institutionalism, that markets themselves provide the needed normative guidance. This position is not greatly different from the Calvinist doctrine that economic success, especially in markets, ethically validates whatever methods brought it about. This amounts to arguing that such companies as Enron are economically proper and ethical just because they have prospered in markets, albeit with considerable government help. A serious flaw in the Buckley's normative economic organization is that it requires individuals to accept and use economic organizations that they may or may not have participated in creating or sustaining. This subtraction from full individual control of this use of economic organization is all the worse because it is not needed for optimum economic cooperation by individuals. As noted here frequently, the positive economic benefits of cooperation through economic organization provide adequate motivation without normative inputs that can only depart from the economic optimizing of individuals.

The Catholic effort to set forth acceptable standards of economic behavior is long standing, beginning most prominently with *"Rerum Novarum*[5]", (New Things), the famed 1891 encyclical of Pope Leo XIII also referred to as *On the Condition of workers.* Pope Leo XIII decried the unjust distribution of income between the working class and the ownership class in the capitalism of his day. However, he strongly opposed state socialism, the form of government popular among most of those who shared his concerns about the plight of working people in capitalism. Forty years later, Pope Pius XI honored the anniversary of Leo's encyclical with *Quadragesimo Anno* (Fortieth Anniversary).[6] Pius XI largely agreed with Leo XIII's views about economic justice but also brought attention to middle level economic organizations, specifically naming labor unions, employer organizations such as syndicates and professional associations as organizations that, with normative input from the Church should provide just economic coordination. Pius XI placed some emphasis on the need for middle-level economic organizations, at least in part to replace the state in guiding economic behavior, leaving it free for its other tasks. Heinrich Pesch, a German Jesuit, writing a five-volume teachers guide to economics published between 1905 and 1923, used "solidarism" as the word for an economic systems in which individuals pursued their goals and treated each other properly under church guidance. French writer Francois Perroux used "communitè" for "ordiné" the Quadragesimo Latin term for the good group, making it a forsighted closeness to the word communication recognized in this book as the basic purpose of economic organization. In a current article in *the national Catholic Weekly* published by Jesuits of the United States, Notre Dame economist Charles K. Wilbur restates the need for ethics as a companion of self-interest in efficient and just markets.[7] Citing Adam Smith and his interpreters, he takes the position that God built into mankind (individuals) not just self-interest and greed but also an "understanding that virtue is a prerequisite for a desirable market society." This view is in agreement with Catholic "natural order" economists and philosophers, but at least somewhat in conflict with both popes Leo XIII and Pius XI, and Pesch as well, all of whom believed that individuals needed outside ethical guidance from the Church. It is also in conflict with this work, which posits that a unified economic theory can and should assume that the benefits of economic cooperation for self-seeking individuals are alone sufficient to build optimum economic organizations.

From this base, Catholic economics developed a broader interest in the characteristics of effective and just economic groups (the "good groups") to arrange economic cooperation in a just industrial society using the vigor of self-seeking individuals combined with economic organization in the form of "Catholic teachings". There has been some insistence that there should be a high degree of consistency between the interest and objectives of the good group and those of its members as individuals. On occasion, Pesch and others have mentioned that ethical and cooperative economic behavior is natural to individuals and God-given. On balance most Catholic economics seems to see the need for both an organizational input provided by the Catholic Church and a natural individual characteristic that limit self-interest for the common good. This is a compromise and contrasts with the position that individuals need only be rational and see the benefits to them of cooperation with others to an extent determined operationally and rigorously by equating the marginal communications costs and benefits of doing so.

There has been no prominent recognition in Catholic economics that the essential purpose of economic organization is to reduce and make manageable the communications costs of cooperation, which as previously noted, is a critical element of both unified theory and a useful economics of economic organizations. Such recognition would show that the nature and extent of each individual's participation in an economic organization must be wholly consistent with that individual's welfare.

Buchanan recognized that self-seeking individuals combine economic organization with markets and also that individuals should have philosophical priority over the economic organizations they use, identified herein as organizational subsidiarity. However, like his law and economics colleagues at George Mason University, he believes that individuals will develop economic institutions and organizations from their market operations and choices instead of being created rationally by individuals seeking to reduce their costs of communications. Exactly how optimum economic organizations are created and kept exactly as best serve its individuals is not clear. Buchanan's approach certainly lacks the rigor of the approach in this book, which follows equal marginal analysis in setting a specific point at which economic organization will be used in comparison with other options and does so in each dimension in which economic cooperation is expanded. At times Buchanan considers that all economic institutions and organizations are essentially governmental, thus ignoring the middle-level economic organizations that are voluntarily and spontaneously created largely by private individuals. But he argues also that economic theory must define optimization as that of the individual and, with Kenneth Arrow, refuses to accept optimizing from the viewpoint of a majority or plurality as basis for successful and lasting economic organizations, a key point made in this book. His insistence upon the individual can be incorporated in the theory of economic organization only by recognizing that individuals use economic organization as an option available to them to reduce the cost of communication insofar as the value of increased cooperation justifies the costs.

In their 2009 book, Akerlof and Shiller[8] abandon economics in favor of psychology and social psychology at the point at which individuals' behaviors cease to be totally self-serving. Because they move so quickly to psychology, they do not grant any credibility at all to the principle that a rational individual will see personal benefit in economically cooperating with other individuals. There is also virtually no mention of the costs of communications, although one can infer that those costs eventually limit the speed and strength of rumor-based collapses in previously established financial arrangements. The authors extend "run-on-the-bank" explanations to failures of the powerful and basically sound non-bank financial institutions.

There can be little doubt that psychology plays a role in the many major financial collapses chronicled by Akerlof and Shiller. However, as the authors note in their discussion of Ponzi schemes, negative public psychology about financial failures are more often the result rather than the cause of failures of major financial institutions. With particular relevance to business investment spending, a critically important variable in Keynesian thought, Akerlof and Shiller point to depressed "animal spirits" as the cause of the unwillingness of businesses to increase investment spending to end a recession. But there is a much better explanation. Whatever the cause of recessions and especially fear that they will worsen, they are accompanied by a decrease in consumption spending and thereby of sales. This in its turn causes a decrease in the use of plant and other tools of production. Why then should businesses be expected to spend for new capital equipment when they already have large unused capacity, particularly when there is no expectation that sales will increase from their currently depressed level? It is true that the expectation in regard to future sales may be psychologically influenced, but again, this is a result not a cause of depressed capital spending. Keynesian economists, and Keynes himself, recognized the reluctance of private businesses to increase investment spending in a recession, causing them to advocate increased in government spending. Akerloff and Shiller correctly recognize that lowered interest rates are not likely to cause an increase in private investment spending, blaming it on depressed animal spirits. A better explanation is that uncertainties about the profitability of payback for additional capital equipment threatens the survival of the business involved or at least the survival in control of its leadership.

In a free society, spontaneously created economic organizations and their usages are numerous, highly varied, flexible and rapidly responsive to changes in both general and industry-specific economic conditions. Many, including those in very important housing construction, are mostly local. Other business organizations, some of which are surprisingly small, are selling their products nationally and/or internationally. They include huge international corporations, both long-lived and relatively new. Ideally economic organizations are spontaneously formed when needed and are eliminated by competition when no longer needed. The very large number of economic organizations being formed and dying continuously can and should be regarded as a type of free markets. Therefore, those who insist that the markets alone should be trusted to arrange optimum economic cooperation are correct, provided that markets are defined to include separate free and vigorous markets for spontaneously formed and mortal economic organizations. On this volatile stage, the movement of nation-states in and out of economic organizations and functions is natural and productive, differing according to circumstances such as war or peace, economic stability or recession, etc.

A corollary of the need for truth in the formation and functioning of economic organizations is that information security systems that impede transfer of information to individuals participating in an economic organization created to reduce information costs are inherently faulted, directly preventing the communication essential to optimum combinations of economic organization and markets. Outlandish and unearned economic gains that are usually and legally attributed to the use of inside information are more properly attributed to the secrecy systems that make them possible. On the practical side, it is hard to understand why executives all too commonly hire at premium pay assistants to help them achieve their objectives and then egocentrically refuse to communicate these objectives to them so they can help to realize them. The management of information on a "need to know" basis could well be the most important cause of business and government waste and lost profit opportunities.

For the many organizations that are only partially economic, the principles set forth here apply only to the part of their operations and position that is actually economic. Proper economic activity for mixed function organizations is limited to those that benefit its participants economically and known by them to do so. A mixed-function organization that uses its overall power and size to function economically beyond the scope of a similarly positioned independent economic organization is a prostitution of the natural processes of human economic cooperation. It can provide great gains to a minority of participants at the expense of other participants and the economy as a whole. This rule applies to nation states and means that their economic actions practicably should be limited to those that have total or near total support of the populations.

Thus far the errors of omission and commission in the treatment of economic organization in economic theory are regrettable, serious and fatal to economics as a credible and unified discipline. More importantly however, is a related unfortunate misuse of economic theory: the use of free market justifications to defend economic organizations without an attending insistence that they meet their two essential characteristics: that they be based on complete truth and open information, and that they maintain susidiarity, giving complete priority over themselves to each and every participating individual.

3
Utopian Communities as Economic Organization

UTOPIAN COMMUNITIES, AS IDEAS AND as experiments, have been numerous and highly diverse in both nature and purpose. However, virtually all of the utopian communities that were actually established have incorporated some kind of communal economic activity, either as initially conceived or eventually, even without a stated economic purpose. In an economics of economic organization, abstracting from the usually present religious and/or anti religious motivations and other non-economic purposes, the utopian ideas and experiments can be seen as communities so small and so structured that the communications costs of economic cooperation are very low.

When, in an economic downturn in a complex society a baker across the street from a shoe repairman needs his shoes repaired while the shoe repairman needs bread, eventually the two of them will trade shoe repairs for bread. Eventually also the scope of cooperation will widen and a leadership will emerge and propose that an economically isolated community committed to economic cooperation be formed. The variations in utopian communities have been more in non-economic than in economic characteristics, with wide differences among them in regard to religion, family structure, and rights of women, sexual practices and other non-economic characteristics. Economically, all are responding to the question: why tolerate community economic problems when we can act as a community to remove them, even if we have other objectives as well?

Utopian communities in the United States were many, some of them famous and some little known largely because of their brief existence. Those of special relevance to economic organization and the manner in which people thought about them include Robert Owen's New Harmony in Indiana, one of the most elaborate and most famous of the rash of such communities in the United States in the first half of the 19th century. Unlike the leaders of many other utopian communities established in America in the 19th and 20th centuries, Robert Owen's was not motivated by religion. Within the limits of the terms in use at the time, he was variously an atheist, an agnostic, and a worshipper of science in an anti-religious way. He was even called an infidel. Owen's activities and projects were not limited to his utopian New Harmony project. He viewed organized religion and even early 19th century society as a whole as corruptors of the cooperation that is natural to individuals. Owen's writings, private business practices and his political advocacies all show a conviction that spontaneous economic cooperation among workers produced results that are best for individuals and best for society as a whole. He essentially proved this to his own satisfaction and to many of his erstwhile critics as well, not at New Harmony but in his considerable success as a benevolent manager of highly successful textile enterprises.

Other especially relevant utopian communities include John Noyes' Oneida in New York, Charles Fourier's phalanxes in France, George and Sophia Ripley's Brook Farm[9] in Massachusetts, and the Mormon United Order Communities in Utah, Nevada and Arizona.[10] In each of these communities markets played a role and there was some type of organized economic cooperation, commonly but not exclusively based on religion or religion-like socially accepted norms.

Initially and for some years, the utopian community at Oneida established radically unconventional marriage and family practices. Later, under strong outside pressures, the community gradually changed into an essentially economic collective enterprise concentrating on making and selling silverware. Oneida became one of the most successful and most enduring of the utopian communities in the United States, arguably because it ultimately became wholly an economic community with the cooperation derived from its small size and good communications. However, in late years, it has ceased manufacturing silverware at Oneida and most recently has announced plans virtually to cease all remaining operations.

Charles Fourier's pattern for his proposed phalanxes was based on transcendentalism, with strong emphasis on the full realization of the intellectual and emotional potential of individuals through the natural inclination of individuals to work in harmony with one another. Brook Farm began as a declared offshoot of Fourier's teachings, and despite its foundation by a minister and his wife was officially non-religious. The land used by Brook Farm was purchased for the purpose of establishing there a utopian community, but proved to have poor soil and incapable of agriculturally supporting the community. The community's main source of income became education, but from its founding to its end, Brook Farm remained non-viable economically, a situation greatly aggravated by a fire that destroyed its uninsured main building.

While Brook Farm became known worldwide and attracted paying visitors (including Robert Owen), it failed to achieve its transcendental expectation of harmony through a combination of ennobled manual labor and intellectual living, even for most of its strongest initial supporters. For an economics of economic organization, the Brook Farm experience appears to be yet another demonstration that shirking responsibility to one's community or faithfully meeting community responsibilities appears to be an individual characteristic little influenced by organizational environments.

In contrast to the non-religion origins of New Harmony and many other utopian communities the Mormon United Order communities in Utah, Arizona and Nevada were strongly religiously motivated and declaredly so. In his later years, long-time Mormon leader Brigham Young came to believe that his leadership had become inadequately religious. Following an idea of Mormonism founder Joseph Smith, he sought to establish "United Order" communalities that shared assets, economic activity, child-rearing and many other parts of life, bringing with it religious devotion, a willingness to share with others and general moral improvement of individuals. In practice, however, the United Order communalities varied considerably in the nature and degree of communal activity. The Mormon religion had no clerics, as such, and although there were lay bishops at local levels, there was not a hierarchy of full-time church officials able and willing to enforce consistency among geographically dispersed United Order communities.

Bunkervile in Nevada is particularly interesting because its two founders, Bishops Bunker and Bishop Leavitt, had been leaders of earlier failed United Order communities that pooled all assets of their constituent families into their communal organizations. In their second try of the United Order at Bunkerville, the leaders reduced the fraction of assets pooled by members to 40%, a number probably closer to the fraction of assets in which there was a true common economic interest.

Eventually, virtually all utopian communities failed or survived only in radically modified form, especially in respect to economic affairs. Despite the investment of almost all of Robert Owen's considerable fortune, New Harmony, Indiana, as originally conceived and structured, lasted less than four years. Brook Farm, plagued by debt throughout its existence survived for only about six years. Bunkerville, despite the modifications of United Order form at its beginning, officially lasted only for some three years, although some important elements of economic cooperation, such as the irrigation system, were continued unofficially and in different form for many years after the legal dissolution of the United Order community itself.

The most common reason for failure given by the leaders and the participating members of most utopian communities was that the communities were built on an unrealistic assumption that living in a community dedicated to cooperation, sometimes even with strong religious guidance, would make people behave less selfishly. In a sense, this implies a belief that individuals must compromise their "economic man" behavior for the good of society, a direct conflict with the fundamental assumptions at the core of economics. It usually appeared from the many chronicles of Mormon family members living in United Order communities that those who would work and "do their share" before joining in a utopian community would do so afterward, while those who avoided community work before joining continued to shirk once in a community that assumed that they would not do so. Thus, the United Order lesson supports that of Brook Farm that the willingness to cooperate with others mostly resides within individuals rather than in an imposed political or religious structure, however strong and backed by religion. In this view, contrasting with that of Owen, individuals are not naturally cooperative, or at least only diversely so, thereby requiring unprecedented religious or other authoritarian guidance to cooperate and compromise their economic-man natures.

On balance, the view that economic cooperation requires compromises with self interest, was prominent in utopian thought. A closely related methodological position is that economic cooperation must be normatively established in reality and abstracted from in positive economics. As has been shown in the last chapter, this is a continuing view, even in those schools of economic thought that recognize the essentiality of economic organization to optimum economic cooperation.

The basic conflict of views about the cooperative nature of man or the lack thereof is as old as mankind and continuing in many forms. However, the point is moot for economic theory recognizing that rational individuals use economic organization to reduce the costs of communication and economic cooperation that benefits them as individuals. For economic theory that is most useful in the modern world, it matters not at all if individuals are naturally cooperative. What matters instead is that economics assumes that rational individuals equate at the margin expenditures on communication with the benefits of economic cooperation brought by communication. More generally and restating, the history of utopian experiments is important to economics, not because it settles the age-old question of whether or not individuals are naturally cooperative, but because utopian communities, intentionally or not, were attempts to make manageable the costs of communication that determines the nature and degree of economic cooperation among rational self-seeking individuals.

4
Communications Costs and Microeconomics

THIS CHAPTER AND THE NEXT two present examples of revisions in economic theory needed to recognize and incorporate communications costs and economic organization. Because communications costs and economic organization are critically important but largely ignored throughout economics even a comprehensive listing of the needed changes is beyond a reasonable scope of this book. However, a few important examples can be included and discussed to stimulate interest. The examples presented in this chapter are from microeconomics. Chapters 5 and 6 provide examples of changes needed respectively in macroeconomics and international economics.

A first revision of microeconomics concerns supply or more exactly suppliers. One of the founding principles of the famous competitive supply and demand model is that suppliers have no monopoly power. However, to consider a commodity market, even a corn farmer four miles east of Rochelle, Illinois has a monopoly on corn at that particular geographical point and point in time when the corn is ripe. Under the economic-man assumption, any seller in any market will rationally take advantage of whatever monopoly power he has, however small. That is, he will do so unless the costs exceed the benefits of doing so, in which case he will send his output to a so-called competitive market. The competitive market thus exists only because of communications costs. The theory of markets with its competitively determined price and quantity sold must recognize communications costs because it cannot exist without them. This extension of price theory may be of little use in the study of the huge commodity or stock markets, but in respect to many other markets, it becomes increasingly useful in specifying an exact point at which sellers will cease exercising their monopoly advantage and become price takers in a competitive market. The specified point is where the marginal costs of communication equals the marginal benefits from extending trade both for individuals and for society as a whole. The sometimes used argument that the existence of just one additional seller prevents monopoly just as well as many sellers is rigorously refuted by the insertion of communications costs. The increased communications costs in the many sellers case terminates monopoly action at an earlier and different point than that of the two-seller case.

The grading of goods provides a second example of a needed change in microeconomic theory. Adding communications costs and economic organization to the analysis of the grading of goods provides an otherwise missing specification of the optimum number of grades of a good. Grading is based on a very realistic assumption of ubiquitous variation among units of a good. No bushel of wheat is exactly the same in weight or BTU as any other bushel of wheat. Within a single bushel of wheat, no grain is the same as any other. However, if there were no communications costs, full exploitation of the benefits of trade, i.e., the benefits of economic cooperation, requires that each grain of wheat be sold separately at a separate price. With communications costs, the costs of knowing about the variations in bushels or grains limits the extent to which buyers and sellers can exploit the advantages of trading. More formally and fully stated, rational wheat selling requires that the number of grades be increased up to the point at which their marginal costs equals the marginal benefits of exploiting the advantages of increased economic cooperation. Grading represents a compromise that can be identified in ordinary business language with some precision. The more the categories in grading, the more the gain from trading, and this is true not just for buyers and sellers but for society as well. However, the more the categories, the greater the cost, so in theory cost-benefit applies.

Recognition of optimum grading in economic theory allows business practices and statements about them to avoid charges of unfairness based on different prices charged different people for what appears to be the same goods. Air passenger pricing is a good example.

There are officially just three categories of trip pricing: coach, business class and first class, and by and large, the traveling public has come to accept them as different levels of service. But there are a number of different pricing categories for each of the three basic categories, including those for senior citizens, students, frequent fliers, travelers who are airline employees or their relatives, travelers making early reservation and innumerable recipients of special fares or free flights offered by airlines or credit card companies. A portion of this variation apparently was inherited from the long period in which there was effectively no meaningful price competition in air travel. Whatever the cause, grading of goods as a method of increasing the individual gains and the social gains from trade is often poorly explained and justified to using consumers.

Grading involves price discrimination in the minds of those who do not recognize that once grading is established, the goods sold at different prices are different goods. A good example is the well-known case of the unhappy passenger who discovers that the student sitting next to him paid a price less than half that which he paid for the same service. The student, however, was able to purchase his seat on a last-minute basis, and the seat would have been empty had he not been able to revise his schedule so that he could use it. Unlike the full-fare passenger, the student was exposed to the probability that he would not have a seat and was willing to accept that. The two seats were different services and rationally priced separately for the benefit of both passengers and society as a whole.

A third example of the very useful changes in microeconomics that can come from better treatment of communications cost and economic organization concerns the assumption of increasing costs. The competitive supply and demand model states that the higher the price the greater the quantity offered for sale. The picture given is that in producing any good, ingredients and labor used first are those most suitable to the purpose and therefore the cheapest. Additional output requires the use of less suitable inputs and therefore additional output requires higher prices.

A parallel assumption is that the higher the price, the smaller the quantity demanded. Together the two assumptions make possible the supply and demand model that states that there will be a single price and a single quantity sold for any good offered in a competitive market. How then can there be systematic and pervasive quantity discounts with lower prices granted as larger quantities are bought? A closely related question asks how its large volumes of goods sold enables Wal-Mart to offer its goods at prices below those of its competitors There is no answer for these question in mainstream microeconomics as it is. However, once communications costs and economic organization are added to the theory, the answers to such questions are simple and straightforward. Communications costs can be so large as a fraction of total costs, that they outweigh all other costs, particularly in retailing, so that sellers offering quantity discounts decrease costs. It is tempting at this point to use the concept of sunk costs to explain how competition can reduce prices to those that just cover variable costs or even lower if objectives have changed from maximizing profits to gaining ever larger shares of the market. However, the concepts of sunk costs refers to costs fixed in time and unchangeable in each price setting or price taking, whereas the process of balancing markets with economic organization to maximize economic cooperation is continuous. There can be no situation in which investment in communications cost is not recovered as part of the operation of the continuously operating market for economic organizations. The matter can be approached another way: the investment made in communications costs and/or economic organization is itself a variable cost made so in the market for economic organizations that creates, sustains and/or destroys those organizations as necessary to maximize individual welfare.

Practical use of a rational theory of economic organization at the nation-state level would eliminate policies and actions based on national economic aggregates, averages, and rates, all of which are abstractions at the national level and unmanageable by maximizing individuals. Among the least useful aggregates is the money supply in any of it several formulations. Individuals cannot respond to M1, M2, M3 or any of the other formulations advanced by those who seek to find a variable that will validate the money supply as the one and only variable usable in managing the national economy.

Rates of national economic growth that identify increased military expenditures as economic growth and expenditures to repair hurricane damage are equally beyond individual contemplation and computation in personal optimizations. On the other hand, real economic progress in the form of improved quality of goods and services is ignored in computing gross domestic product even though it definitely can be perceived by optimizing individuals.

5
Communications Costs, Economic Organization and Macroeconomics

BORN OF THE FINANCIAL CRISES of the Fall of 2008 and the ensuing World recession, macroeconomics is admittedly "at difficult juncture"[11] This chapter offers a palliative, presenting examples of changes in macroeconomics required to incorporate communications costs and economic organization into the macroeconomic theory making it once again a defensible base for rational economic ideology and policy. The first example addresses the essence of macroeconomics, its use of aggregates such as the money supply, aggregate demand and aggregate supply and national rates such as interest rates and unemployment. However, from the viewpoint of the individuals whose choices add up to economic aggregates, averages and national rates are abstractions. The individual whose economic posture in all respects is exactly average is rare indeed, and each individual must use his own amounts and values and not national aggregates, averages or rates in optimizing his economic actions. Only thus, can a self-seeking individual optimize his use of economic cooperation.

While neither individuals nor a national monetary authority can rationally integrate M1, M2, M3 or other officially published quantities of money into individual efforts to optimize economic cooperation, individuals can adjust their levels of economic organization and the liquidity of their portfolios in such manner as to balance their marginal communications costs with the marginal gains they obtain from economic cooperation. This is something only individuals can do. The Keynesian models still apply, but the level of decision on such matters as business investment spending must be low enough so that individuals can know and consider moneyness of all assets rather than just the total of a few assets arbitrarily selected to empirically validate various hypotheses about the importance of the quantity of money and interest rates on investment spending.

There are several obvious and important relationships between an economy as a whole and communications. One is that the societal benefits of economic cooperation are inversely related to the general cost of communication. Borrowing from the physical sciences, a decrease in the cost of communication such as that caused by a major improvement in technology is analogous to an increase in the viscosity of a fluid. Contacts among things floating in the fluid become easier and more frequent. The better the technology of communications the cheaper are the benefits of cooperation among individuals, and the greater those benefits will be. More simply, society could be viewed as analogous to a pool of molasses, with individuals swimming in it having great difficulty in swimming to contact other individuals. As water is added and the molasses becomes thinner, there is a reduction in communications costs and the number of contacts among individuals during any time period is greatly increased with gains both for the individuals and for society as a whole.

The classical model of social savings and capital investment uses the marginal efficiency of capital as the basis of the demand for investment funds. Supply of funds is provided by consumers/savers who will defer consumption for a period of time if they can thereby consume more later. Those who spend for capital equipment, i.e., those who borrow capital funds are presumed to have investment opportunities with different rates of return. Different consumers have different preferences for current goods and therefore there are different amounts offered for investment at different rates of interest. In the market for investment funds, the rate of interest equates the quantity supplied and the quantity demanded for investment funds. The reverse is also true. The marginal efficiency of capital in general and the consumer time preference for goods in general (the "agio on present goods" in classical economics) determine the rate of interest. This rate of interest might be well called the "natural" rate of interest on the argument that the determinants on both the supply and demand sides are deep-seated characteristics of an economy, so that when corrected for inflation interest rates will be at or near this natural rate. Considering stability still further and excepting recessions, the savings rate is probably more stable than the marginal efficiency of capital, meaning that the rate toward which real interest rates will trend is the marginal efficiency of capital

What then is to be made of the quantity of money as the determinant of interest rates, and the related assignment to a central bank the task of influencing interest rates, investment spending and thereby prices, output and employment? The natural question that follows is, "does saving increase income by adding capital and thereby increasing labor productivity? (The classical economics view is that it does) or does increased saving reduce and eventually cut off the multiplied stream of income that comes from an increase in investment spending (The Keynesian view)? The answer is that investment does require saving, but from income created by investment spending itself.

Business demand for investment funds is not very responsive to changes in interest rates, realistically or even theoretically, especially when most needed in recessions, nor should they be, given the uncertainties of general business conditions, with percentage variation in sales that dwarf changes in interest rates as determinants of profits and losses. Typically, there is a high level of uncertainty as to whether the investment projects will succeed at all, but with an expectation that if they do succeed, they will return the investment in them within a very short time. With the option of economic organization, rational investors in businesses will seek contracts that will keep them functioning over a reasonable range of business conditions. Additionally, there are objectives in investment spending other than profits. One is the expansion of market share, to which executive pay and even survival is often tied. Another non-profit goal is the sense of progress respected even by those who do not necessarily agree on the particular dimension of progress.

On the consumer/saver side, both realistically and theoretically, individual savings are a residual with little or any responsiveness to changes in the interest rate. Given the uncertainty in their worlds, rational individuals who are not saving at five percent interest will not save at ten percent. The incentive of being able to consume five percent more a year from now is just not there, given the common rates of change in individual circumstances. Rather than responding to changes in the interest rate, consumer/savers are likely to use economic organization to reduce the uncertainties in their lives through a more secure employment or a more stable pension plan.

Keynes and his followers believed that, at least under the extreme conditions of the Great Depression, investment by private industry could not be stimulated by reductions in interest rate or any other monetary mechanism such as increased availability of credit. After all, a business not using a large part of its capacity is not likely to borrow to add to capacity, no matter how low the interest rate or how available is credit. Even businesses that agreed with society's need for increased investment spending could not afford to begin it and had no responsibility to do so. The Keynesians therefore advocated increases in spending by government, which, in the views of many, did have a responsibility for economic conditions. This view was captured and made a matter of law in the United States with the Full Employment Act of 1946. Nevertheless, there remained opposition to deficit spending by government as a means of ending recessions. The common opposition is captured in the oft-spoken view that, "I have to reduce my spending in a recession, why shouldn't government have to do the same?"

The answer to the preceding question is not forthcoming from conventional economics, which is based fundamentally on scarcity, and certainly, if such events as floods or drought cause "hard times", government should reduce its spending and use of scarce resources. But when the recession is caused by deficiencies in demand, then the option of economic organization at the level of the nation-state could well be best for society and for individuals. That action could be the construction of needed new government buildings or national defense weaponry using facilities and labor that otherwise would be idle and wasted. However, the rules derived from economic theory relating economic cooperation to communication must be followed, and the governmental projects selected should be those selected with both truth and open information and obvious benefits to individuals. As seen in Chapter 3 on utopian dreams, economic cooperation may or may not be as natural to individuals as selfishness of economic-man, who may or may not recognize that all economic goals, whether selfish or unselfish, must be reached through a combination of markets and economic organization.

In an elaboration Keynesians, although not Keynes himself, developed a model that relates the equality of investment spending (I) and savings (S) and the equality of the supply of money (M) and the demand for money to hold (L) to the interest rate and income. Changes in any one of the four variables will alter interest rates and income, but the variable usually presumed to be available to the nation-state's managers of the economy is the quantity of money. As is the case with other quantity of money models, there is a problem with money substitutes. The model considers that money pays no interest but is totally liquid by definition while other financial assets such as bonds and savings accounts do pay interest, but are not liquid at all. Higher rates cause individuals to exchange money in their portfolios for interest-bearing wealth. Opposing this tendency, the demand for money balances is presumed to be increased by higher incomes, effectively considering that higher incomes reflect a need for greater liquidity. But many if not most of the interest-bearing alternatives to money are themselves highly liquid. For rational use, this model would require degrees of liquidity along a scale of the communications costs of changing other financial assets to money.

The communications cost-economic organization approach presumes that individuals would determine the mixture of money and interest-bearing substitutes considering their individual risk preferences, the probabilities of relevant changes in the economy and the costs and benefits of changing various assets to others with different costs and benefits. Throughout the economic scene, economic organization, including contracting to reduce risks, offers for individuals alternatives to market risk. It is impossible for a nation-state manager of the economy to know even one individual's risk preferences, much less everyone's preferences, and in consequence, there is no possibility of rationally changing the money supply to induce optimum changes in the interest rate and through them changes in output, employment, economic growth and prices.

There is an older model called the equation of exchange that advocates use of the money supply in unspecified form to advocate monetary control of the economy. The model posits a spending total by multiplying the quantity of money by its velocity, the average number of times each unit of money is spent in a particular period of time. The resulting total expenditure is equated to the total value of output consisting of the total value of national output at its prices. The quantity of money, whatever it is, must turn over enough times to buy the national output. Advocates argue that on average people are paid monthly but spread their spending of income over the month. Thus, a family paid $3,000 on the first of the month will have $3,000 in money on the first of the month and zero in money at the end of the month, with an average money balance of $1,500. The ratio of money to total income is $1,500 divided by $3,000, which is equal to one-half. On average each dollar must be spent twice, so that the velocity of money is two. There is no possibility and no need to try to follow each dollar as it is spent multiple times; it is necessary only to measure the money supply and divide it by the value of national product, and then invert it to obtain the velocity of money. But there is really no need to do even that calculation. Proponents argue that pay periods are a cultural phenomenon that remains the same year after year, and therefore, the velocity of money is stable. In consequence, the total value of output must vary directly and proportionately with the quantity of money. Now, if output is also stable, as it would be if the economy were at capacity and remaining so, then the level of prices must depend wholly on the quantity of money. If, on the other hand, prices are stable, then output and employment must depend wholly on the quantity of money. Management of the economy is conceptually simple. If there is inflation reduce the money supply. If there is unemployment, increase the money supply. However, lags and leads in the economy make this difficult in practice, so many monetarists recommend that the money supply be increased rigidly at the long range rate of growth in real output.

Analysis of the equation of exchange in terms of communications costs and economic organization begins with a reiteration of a point made in Chapter 2. Like all monetarist solutions, both the I=S, L=M model and the equation of exchange treat all or at least a majority of individuals in the economy as average. In fact an individual whose wants, risk preferences and other characteristics relevant to money are exactly average is a very rare individual indeed. Chapter 2 presents the concept of subsidiarity with the covenant that optimum economic organizations must benefit each individual in every aspect of that individual's participation. Policies and actions that are designed for the average participant or a majority of participants cannot provide optimum economic cooperation. A best fit of relationships is provided not by treating all individuals as average or the same as a majority, but by allowing each individual to shop his participation to his own desires and needs.

The history of civilization is paralleled by the history of money, and money is a creature of economic organization. The traditionally recognized primary function of money as a medium of exchange is a pure example of the use of economic organization to reduce the communications costs of economic cooperation. It avoids the costs of searching for a double coincidence of wants. Like language money will emerge as part of the natural order in any group of individuals who seek to better their lots through economic cooperation.

Any and all goods have some moneyness in that they can be exchanged for other goods, albeit at some communications cost, so that moneyness of a good could well be defined as the average communications cost of exchanging that good for other goods that are not money. There is nothing that cannot serve as money, and it need not have any intrinsic value. Presently most of that which is officially recognized as money by nation-states or combinations thereof consists of bookkeeping entries of debt to depositors. Its sole requirement for existence as money is that it be acceptable to the individuals using it. Monies proclaimed as such by nation-states have different levels of acceptance by individuals depending to an important extent on the perceived stability of the issuing government. But there are exceptions. The old Austria-Hungarian Thaler in which long established respect and silver content have caused it to be accepted in bazaars for decades after the demise of the issuing government. Also, a century and more ago notes issued by some U.S. national banks have continued in use after the banks ceased to exist. There are even productive uses of bills known by the users to be counterfeit.

Money is an imperfect creature of economic organization. If money were perfect, individuals would see through to and discount its total effects making it neutral. Thus, money has its effects only because of its imperfections as economic organization, and the failures of money markets to require truth and open information. For most people income comes as the receipt of money for their work or as returns on investments. It is easy to reverse the relationship and consider any receipt of additional money to be income. However, income is an increase in real wealth, and there are many receipts of money that do not add to wealth. The exchange of a non-money asset for money, an ordinary sale, increases an individual's money holdings, but does not add anything to individual or societal wealth, instead just changing its form for the individual but not for society. If a good is sold for more that was paid for it, there is an accounting profit from its sale. But just before the sale the asset was already worth the price it brought, so the sale itself left total wealth, as it was producing no income. There was income, of course, but it was produced over the period the asset was held.

It is not hard to understand why there is much confusion about balanced budgets. A budget can be balanced as economists see it, but deeply in deficit on a cash flow basis. For example, if the Federal Government builds housing on a military base, the cost is added to expenses adding to the budget deficit and to the national debt. But the government now has the base housing equal in value to its cost, and so the government's wealth is unchanged and there is no addition to the deficit. However, the cost of constructing the housing, while ultimately repaid from rents, must be paid currently, from either taxes or borrowing. The most-used governmental balance of the budget equates total expenditures with total revenues, mostly from taxes, so the expenditure for the base housing result in a much-deplored increase in a deficit, although it may well be good business. Following a rational economics of economic organization, the government can avoid the contribution to its deficit by having a private company contract for the housing and its financing. The company can simply borrow from banks, who thereby create the money needed to build the housing. There will be critics of the program who, based on their personal experiences, will ask, "Where the money is going to come from?" The answer is that it is created by bank lending. When the private builder eventually repays the loan from rents, the money supply is reduced by the amount of the loan. In real terms, the housing is an increase in national wealth that involved money but only as a communications device. The needed increase in base housing also could have been created by contracting with the future users of base housing, who would commit a stream of future payments in exchange for a commitment to provide housing for them wherever they may be stationed. The simple base housing example illustrates how economic organization, given the flexibility and dedication to individual benefits it has when optimally used, can substitute approvable local economic organization for economic organization at the nation-state level for which approval is not forthcoming because negative net money flows are treated as deficits.

A last example of the needed changes in macroeconomics concerns again the relationship between keeping money and savings as increases in wealth. At the basics of the Keynesian analysis, increased capital spending by business results in a multiplied increase in total income by initiating a stream of expenditures. That is, a dollar spent on a new factory or an increase in inventory will be received and spent again except for the part that the recipient saves. Those receiving this second round of spending will spend it again keeping back a fraction of it in savings. In the end, the savings will finally bring the spending stream to a halt. The more people hold back in savings, the sooner the income stream will stop and the less total spending will be. Since action must always take place from the present position, economists are interested in the fraction of new spending that will be saved, which they call the marginal propensity to save. Accordingly the total new spending that will result from each dollar of new spending is equal to the reciprocal of the marginal propensity to spend, known as the Keynesian multiplier. The result is that the larger the fraction of their incomes people save the smaller will be the multiplier and the larger will be the amount businesses or government must spend to create a given increase in total income. There is an apparent conflict with the long-established classical model previously discussed that shows that the less a society consumes of its output, and therefore the larger its savings, the greater will be societal capital and productivity and the wealthier the society will become.

The conflict betweens the classical and the Keynesian view is readily resolved with attention to economic organization. The Keynesian analysis addresses flow of money, which results in multiplied real increases in capital and future well-being of individual and society as a whole. However, investment spending by borrowing is not the whole of investment spending, either realistically in modern capitalism or theoretically once economic organization is recognized. Economic organization can finance investment spending not just from borrowing but also in whole or in part from retained earnings, an organizational mechanism available to individuals who may see uncertainty as too great to risk survival by borrowing. Alternatively, investment may be influenced not by attractive marginal efficiency of capital and profits but by chief executive officers pursuing larger market shares. Investment spending can be financed by new issues of stock, bypassing interest rates and the risk of enterprise failure because of inability to make interest payments. Still a third method of organizational business investment spending by entities is the purchase of already existing facilities often through mergers. In the last method, there is no addition to social capital, and no investment in the view of classical economics, although there may be borrowing at interest or issuance of common stock.

The management of a nation-state's economic affairs inevitably involves economic aggregates and averages, which have somewhat subtle implications in the light of the economics of economic organization with its emphasis on communications costs. Both aggregates and averages are abstractions in that they are not regularly in the experience of individuals in a free market economy. In fact and in any natural order, arithmetic averages are very rare indeed, and the sum of individual values becomes more and more abstract as numbers become larger. It would be fair to state that individuals in a nation-state do not meaningfully share a particular value of the nation's gross domestic product as a national goal. They can and do, however, share in a community investment spending program to save a factory in a community that depends on that factory for a major contribution to its economic base. Alternatively, in another dimension individuals may share in a physicians organization for the promotion of computerized patient records to which individual physicians can relate.

The relationships between organization and abstraction are little developed in economic theory but very promising. It is useful to consider certain words and/or concepts as cases in which limiting abstraction is appropriate. Such a concept is "national environmentalism." Individuals know what it means, and there is some general sense of responsiveness of individuals to the need to turn off a fan or a light when vacating a room. However, such responsiveness is modest in comparison with the gain in environmental consciousness from active individual action in which the results are seen. For example, individuals that are made aware of butterflies and provide butterfly friendly plants in their yards, can be expected to cause many people to become interested in the insect world in general and then on to the animal kingdom in general and finally on to the environment in general. If such patterns are begun and pursued at every step with transparency and individualism, the overall result is organization meeting the important criteria of truth, open information and the subsidiarity of any organized efforts to serve the interests of its members. Attempts to overenlarge the scope of an organization will be unproductive. With respect to butterflies in the United States for example, state-level organization is probably more productive of environmental consciousness than a national effort.

From the viewpoint of economic theory, the economic man is precluded by his rationality from using economic aggregates in his optimizing decisions. Aggregates simply do not fit his circumstances. A particularly important difference between an average of individuals greatly exceeds variation in their average, and it is individual variation that establishes the risk level in investment spending, for example. Collective risk decisions made on behalf of multiple individuals must address individual risks not average risks. Otherwise the economic-man assumption is theoretical error. With that, a unified economic theory is precluded.

Another example of the application of the theory here to money in markets is a variation of the "ticket" and commodity theories of money, as used in an idealized utopian community. In a situation that is as accurate historically as it is fictional, visualize the founding of a small isolated pioneer community in the 19th century western United States. There is a need for housing and a sawmill is established to provide the necessary lumber. But the community is isolated, having cut itself off from the rest of society to avoid persecution for unusual religious beliefs and also to keep its economy simple. Furthermore, the newly established community has very high unemployment. The owner/operator of the sawmill hires most of the unemployed in the community, but having no money and no access to any, pays his labor by giving them one ticket for each hour worked in the mill. The tickets are redeemable in lumber. Very soon after the issuance of lumber mill tickets, some of them begin to be traded for groceries or other non-lumber goods.

Enticed by a ticket bonus, some workers who do not plan to build for a substantial period of time, leave at least part of their earned tickets with the mill owner, who uses them to make advance payments to selected workers who want to build now but have not accumulated enough lumber tickets to do so. The total number of tickets issued is not allowed to exceed the amount of lumber produced, and everyone in the community knows this. The lumber mill has become a bank, but not necessarily a monopoly in all bank functions. Individuals are free to contact each other and make bargains in which those workers not ready to use their earned lumber can nevertheless take the tickets for it and transfer them to the highest bidder directly, incurring however, the communications cost of finding that bidder. As individuals choose between using the mill/bank and hustling for direct deals, they are optimizing their mixture of economic organization and markets as set forth in Chapter 2.

The second extreme is in many respects the opposite of the previously described community small enough and isolated enough so that individuals can see through to final effects and use that information in optimizing their cooperation. Essentially an idealized part of a socialist planned economy, this second extreme, although never achieved even in meaningful part, was given the name "zero rachun" (zero balances) in Yugoslavia before its break up. The idealized system provided that at the end of each business day, a totally computerized economy would clear all balances and obligations, and no enterprise, government entity or any other organization would have any money balances when the clearing was finished. Basically, the system would make money totally neutral, or more accurately, non-existent in favor of organizational arrangements that ignore the moneyness of asset i.e., the inverse of communications cost of converting them to the "zero rachun" format. As already noted, just as markets cannot exist without some economic organization, economic organization cannot exist rationally without some market usage. And so the dream of zero rachun remained just that, an impossible dream both realistically and theoretically. Still the concept of a constantly clearing debt balances is a sort of "reducto-ad-adsurdum" that reveals the true nature of money as economic organization.

6
International Economic Cooperation, Communication and Organization

INTERNATIONAL ECONOMICS IS PERHAPS THE oldest part of economics. It remains, however, the part of economics in which economists are mostly now in agreement with each other but frequently and persistently in disagreement with non-economists. And the opposition is not just at the popular level, but also in legislative bodies and their lobbyists, among the media, and sometimes in critically relevant elements of government as a whole. The subject areas of the disagreement also is broad, extending alike to international trade, international finance and even to basic economic systems. In respect to time periods and major economic eras such as the industrial revolution and the information systems revolution, popular irrationalities have been ever present and continuing.

Import restriction has been the most persistent of the popularly supported policies opposed by economists. The reasons are many. Confusion of income with money flows is one. Confusion of sales and their increase with profits and investment spending with consumption is another. Strong organization of producers in comparison with the weak almost non-existent organization and political power of consumers is perhaps the most important factor supporting import restrictions. Labor unions, which are part of production but with many members, all of whom are consumers, have largely supported producer positions, rather than defending consumer interests.

There is little media recognition of the damage done to consumer interests by import restrictions, many of which are decades old. Whatever the gains obtained by those protected from foreign competition, they are exceeded by the damage done to others, but this irrefutable principle is seldom cited in media discussions of a specific import restriction. The media and official governmental entities as well use the phrase "deficit in the balance of trade" when the total value of imports exceeds the total value of exports. This usage is a holdover from the era when most nation-states sought to increase their stocks of gold and later reserve currencies and thus to be able to maintain a fixed value of their monies. It has had no meaning since the abandonment of the International Monetary Fund arrangement in 1972. And yet, it is still published by governments and deficits in the balance of trade are widely cited as a governmental failing when it is simply the difference between total exports and total imports of the entire population, not the government. Similarly, the phrase "debtor nation" with its negative connotation refers to a nation-state in which foreigners have invested more than its people have invested in other countries.

Despite the many irrationalities in common perceptions of the international economy, there is progress. The histories of international trade and especially also international finance, when viewed from a rational economics of economic organization show continuing efforts to mix free markets and economic organization. Sometimes achieved and sometimes not, the declared common goal of nations is to share the benefits of economic cooperation at least approximately as if there were no political borders – that is, as the states in the United States, and to a lesser extent have separate political identities but a common economy.

The much-maligned multinational corporations with their widely varying policies and practices and adaptations are at the cutting edge of economic cooperation through different combinations of economic organization and markets. Their often-criticized independence from governmental restriction permits very useful searches for new and effective ways to deliver mutual benefits to individuals in different nation-states. In contrast to foreign aid with its tendencies to yield only temporary benefits, selective development by multinational corporations tend to make them rational and lasting

Economists, and those political leaders who listened to them, reacted to the Great Depression and World War II with US-led establishment of formal international economic organization designed to avoid the pre-WWII virtual shutdown of international economic cooperation.

Included most prominently were the World Bank and the International Monetary Fund established even before World War II ended. The General Agreement on Tariffs and Trade (GATT) was established specifically to reduce import restrictions, and despite fits and starts and frequently successful delays forced by pro-restriction forces, successfully reduced tariffs to about a fourth of their pre-war level. There have since been very important regional cooperative economic agreements, notably the European Union and the North American Free Trade agreement. There have also been important bilateral economic cooperation, most successful of which was the Marshall plan with its US aid to war damaged Europe and Japan.

As noted earlier, the International Monetary arrangement was an attempt to build economic cooperation essentially by making currencies convertible, backed by gold and reserve currencies and thus to function effectively as a single money. By the early 1970's the hardships imposed by maintaining convertibility at fixed rates caused the IMF system to be replaced by floating exchange rates that more easily achieved the goal of improved economic cooperation through the use of better market-tested monies. In terms of economic theory, the move to floating exchange rates represents a useful move from economic organization to the market in the ever-changing adaptive mixture of the two toward better economic cooperation. The fixed exchange rate system for many countries came to be fixed only until the government devalued or revalued its currency, a difficult to predict political decision in contrast to floating rates, determined in the foreign exchange markets that instantly moved currency values toward their purchasing power, except as distorted by managed float.

There has been increased use of managed float in which national governments and their agent central banks buy and sell their currencies to influence their values (to keep them within a certain range in the European Union). This clearly is a move back to economic organization from markets that well might be regarded as a healthy flexibility needed to keep the organization-market mixture at its optimum. As for the IMF, it refused to die when it outlived its usefulness and has since advocated that countries seek rather rigid values for their currencies even at the cost of increased unemployment and weak or even negative economic growth, thus joining the many who continue to pursue goals past their time.

The record has shown that there is much irrationality in the international economy. It has also shown that there is a persistent and successful effort to reduce the irrationalities and establish rational economic cooperation with greater flexibility than is usual for domestic business in most countries. Further, the record also shows that improved communications technology and innovation have greatly expanded international economic cooperation, just as should be expected from an economics of economic organization, with its recognition of the role of communications in economic cooperation. However, the record also shows that financial market participants have too little respect for the two ideologies logically derived from a rational economics of economic organization – truth with open information and subsidiarity that creates economic organizations that best serve the individuals who create and sustain them

7
Economic Organization, Communication, and Financial Markets

THIS CHAPTER CAN ONLY BEGIN the application of the theory of economic organization to the large financial sectors of modern complex economies. Initially it is concerned with of the nature and practices of very large markets, such as Wall Street, the foreign exchange markets and their counterparts, the world over, all as idealized in classical economics and largely also in popular opinion. The much different and seriously defective reality of modern financial markets is then considered in the knowledge that their current defects threaten their very survival despite, and perhaps even because of, governmental aid and controls unprecedented in the long history of law and regulation in financial markets. Additionally, the financial disturbances of the fall of 2008 have caused very serious concern about the shortcomings of economics, and especially macroeconomic theory and its monetarism. Modern concern about economics is at the level of basic postulates and is expressed both by respected economists and in popular media.[12]

The chapter also considers markets such as those for real estate and insurance, which are largely regulated by state governments and in some cases, by private associations. All securities are then considered anew in the light of theory emphasizing communications, truth and subsidiarity, which combine into an ideology derived from and based on a rigorous economics of economic organization.

In classical economic theory, the role of the large markets, common to all types of them, is to combine investments of numerous individuals to finance major productive enterprises guided by capital theory's two governing factors, the marginal productivity of capital on the demand side and the compensation for waiting on the supply side, determining market rates of interest. Although not part of the core of classical economics, trading in already-issued securities is rational and beneficial for both individuals and society insofar, but only insofar, as it improves the fit of individual portfolios to their owners, given individual needs, wants and risk tolerances. But beyond that there are limitations to the rationality for individuals and benefits for society of trading in already-issued securities, One of the most important of these limitations is related specifically to the motives of individuals trading in already-issued securities.

If individuals trade in securities wholly with the purpose of increasing money balances, which is all too often the case, then trading cannot lead to optimization. Money is but one element of organization, and all others must be considered by individuals seeking optimization in their use of organization and markets. The irrationality of trading in already issued securities is greatly aggravated by the virtually complete separation of management and ownership of large modern corporations.

Consistent theory in an economics of economic organization must hold that trading in already-issued securities cannot improve optimization for either individuals or society as a whole if the motive for that trading is reduced wholly to monetary gain. The invisible hand and all that it means require rational consideration, within the limits set by the cost of communications, of all economic options by all individuals, and the all-too-common restriction of motive to "making money in the market" does not meet that criterion. The distortions caused by concentration on increasing stocks of money reached an extreme when increased in stocks of gold and/or reserve currency was the dominant economic motive of middle-ages kingships and in nation-states as recently as in post-World-War II Japan and currently in China.

Individuals motivated wholly by rates of return on investments become vulnerable to insider trading and Ponzi schemes, the driving force for which is high rates of return fueled by new investment attracted by those high rates of return. While Ponzi schemes in which investors lose large amounts of money become well known, there are many programs and projects that come to reward early investors with above-market returns using monies from later investors. Typically there is no enforced disclosure of the source of payments to investors, and if the returns paid to initial investors are not greatly above prevailing rates, they will pass unnoticed. Sometimes funds obtained from new investors are used to reward initial investors without direct money payments to them. This tactic has been used in community-development programs in which rewards to early investors take the form of construction of facilities such as golf courses and club houses that are very useful for initial investors with close by locations, but ever less useful to later investors with more distant locations, even though they provide the money for the facilities. Absent recessions or other factors lowering perimeter sales, such projects can succeed at least modestly without general awareness of their Ponzi elements. Regulation of such programs is usually at the state or local government level, with enforcement by officials who are biased by the hope for increased revenues from community growth. Frequently, all that was necessary to cause the cancellation of the most fraudulent of community development plans was an enforced requirement that advertisements be truthful.

Ponzi schemes and those with important Ponzi elements require that secrecy, not transparency, characterize securities trading. A major weakness of securities markets in general is that legitimate trading has come to be characterized by secrecy with a direct cancellation of the communicating purposes of both markets and economic organization. Secrecy has become a habit, often practiced even when it is damaging, not beneficial, to those who insist on using it.

The evolution of the investment system and particularly its use of money have a long history of public concern and regulation. Popular awareness of the need for truth and open information has led to pervasive regulation of large markets of all types and even to the terminology "fiduciary responsibility" to require especially high standards in communications about other peoples' money placed in trusts.

Yet, the laws and regulations demanding truth and open information have had effects many of which are often opposite to those intended. Believing themselves to be protected by government, investors have believed, when they should not have believed. Also, when regulation is strict and strictly enforced, most of those under it will comply, giving the few who do not comply the largest part of the funds whose owners are determined to receive returns far above prevailing rates, such as those paid by Bernard Madoff in his Ponzi scheme. The solution of more strict regulation thus can be no solution at all, with additional regulation worsening the problems of modern securities markets.

What then is the solution that will bring securities markets into line with Smith's invisible hand? The most commonly suggested is "transparency" But, as noted in Chapter 2, transparency is a vague term, not grounded in accepted economic theory." Surprisingly, there is little recognition of the damage that information security systems do to communication and therefore to economic cooperation. In particular the denial of information until "need to know" is established is absolutely and completely in conflict with trial-and-error marginal equalization of communications costs with marginal benefits. One consequence of the security systems is the very high rewards for use of insider information, which could not exist without those security systems. A second important negative of information security system is their use to hide mistakes of leadership, long characteristic of the military.

Trading in already-issued securities presents different problems. It is formally trading in claims to productive assets, but the goals of most individuals in that market are not increases in production, but increased individual wealth in the form of additions to money balances sometimes in amounts far greater than can be attributed to the values of services an individual could possibly produce or even use. Often the mutuality of trade benefits degenerates into a win-loss situation in which the gains of some are matched by losses of others with no "better-fit" benefits to individuals or society. One much used road to large and consistent gains for an individual in the already-issued securities market is to deceive others or withhold information from them. A common practice is to purchase securities of a poorly performing corporation, then issue a statement that it is about to merge with a highly successful corporation, increasing the value of the weak company's stock. The newly purchased stock is then sold at the higher price generated solely by rumored merger. After this profit taking, the stock in the weak corporation is then sold short, followed by an announcement that the merger is cancelled, depressing the price of the stock, with short-sale profits to the manipulators.

That which is needed in the securities markets is not different from that which is needed throughout the economy – development of a defendable economics of economic organization that complements both microeconomics and macroeconomics. From this, there can emerge widespread business practices that are both respected and optimistic about the economy, economics and economists.

Generalizing from securities markets to economic organization free of geographically constrained nation-states, modern communications technology has opened many non-governmental doors to economic organization. A stamp dealer may have more in common with a stamp dealer in New Zeeland, where he has never been, than he has in common with a next door neighbor, who is an orthopedic surgeon. It is not uncommon for a resident of a modern city in a developed country to have never met his immediate neighbors or even to know their names. There are now many more dimensions of economic cooperation than there were a half-century ago, and the end of the cold war has joined communications technology in opening long-closed doors to economic cooperation.

The irrationalities of common practices in securities markets are not alone. As already mentioned in Chapter 6, national governments and the media still publish balance of trade and balance of payments information, almost a half-century after it lost its relevance in the shift from fixed to floating currency exchange rates. The Federal budget and, except where there is capital budgeting, many budgets at lower levels of government are treated as if government expenditures can add nothing to public wealth. They also treat all expenditures for education as pure current expenditure, failing to recognize their contribution to human capital and to technology. Certainly, the political organizations setting and controlling budgets in the majority of cases do not meet the qualifications of economic organizations usable by individuals in maximizing their well being.

Certain types of businesses in the United States have established traditions of self-regulation to better the reputations and well being of their industries. Academic disciplines, clerics in particular religions, mortuaries and medical associations are good examples. Specialized language is often the binding factor for such organizations, so that their essential characteristic of reducing communications costs is present. Most individuals are members of twenty or thirty formally established economic organizations, without significant conflicts among them. Each individual also belongs, willingly or not, to unorganized economic groups of commonly positioned persons, such as consumers, the elderly, the unemployed and immigrants. Only in very rare cases is an individual's mosaic of economic organizations stable, instead constantly change in number, commonality, function and degree of that individual's involvement. As pointed out in Chapter 2, this is as it should be, despite the common fear of organizational changes and the dubious assertion that some organizations are too big to fail.

A useful closing statement for this book is that, "The education in new economic theory of students, the public in general and even economists is difficult, not because they know so little about it, but because they know so much that isn't so."

Endnotes

1. Santa Clara County v. Southern P.R. Co., 118 {U.S. 1886) (Lexis-Nexis summary) Apparently, the case in wrongfully cited as a Supreme Court decision, since the Court specifically refused to consider the constitutional question about corporations as individuals in that case. The statement that corporations were persons was made only in the headnotes by John C. B. Davis in his capacity as Reporter of the U.S. Supreme Court and should not have been precedent setting in the views of many Court experts. Nonetheless, it has been repeatedly and generally cited as establishing the status of corporations as persons with the rights of persons, including those in the fourteenth amendment.

2. Friedman, Milton Presidential Address, American Economic Association, *American Economic Review* 58 (I):

3. F.A. Hayek, "The "Use of Knowledge in Society," *The American Economic Review*, Sept., 1945 Vol XXV.No. 4 4.

4. Francis H. Buckley *Just Exchange,* Routledge, 2004

5. www.papalencyclicals.net

6. www.papalencyclicals.net

7. Charles K. Wilbur, "Misleading Indicators" *America* Sept. 28, 2009, (Vol 201 No. 7)pp12-15.

8. George A. Akerloff and Robert J. Shiller, *Animal Spirits*, Princeton University Press, 2009.

9. See Wikipedia for a detailed article on Brook Farm

10. A major part of the author's knowledge of the Mormon United Order communities is the result of conversations over many years. The use of sawmill chits as money covered in

Chapter 5 is described as remembered by the descendants of William Wallace Damron, apparently the owner of the sawmill involved.

11.   The words are those of the esteemed Nobel prize winning economist Robert M. Solow . See his comment on the book jacket of *Animal Spirits,* referenced elsewhere

12.   The already cited book *Animal Spirits* by Akerlof and Shiller questions the basic motivational assumptions of the main body of economic thought. The popular media discussion is well represented by two articles in the *New Yorker* magazine. The first, by James Surowicki is "Ratings Downgrade" p 25 of the September 28, 2009 issue supports the conclusion that compromised rating agencies in the securities markets actually add to information problems of the market. The second is John Cassidy's long article "Rational Irrationality" in the *New Yorker* of October 9th, 2009, which attacks the Adam Smith position that self-seeking actions in securities markets by individuals is optimal also for society as a whole.

Index